Classical Music for the Harp

arranged by

Deborah Friou

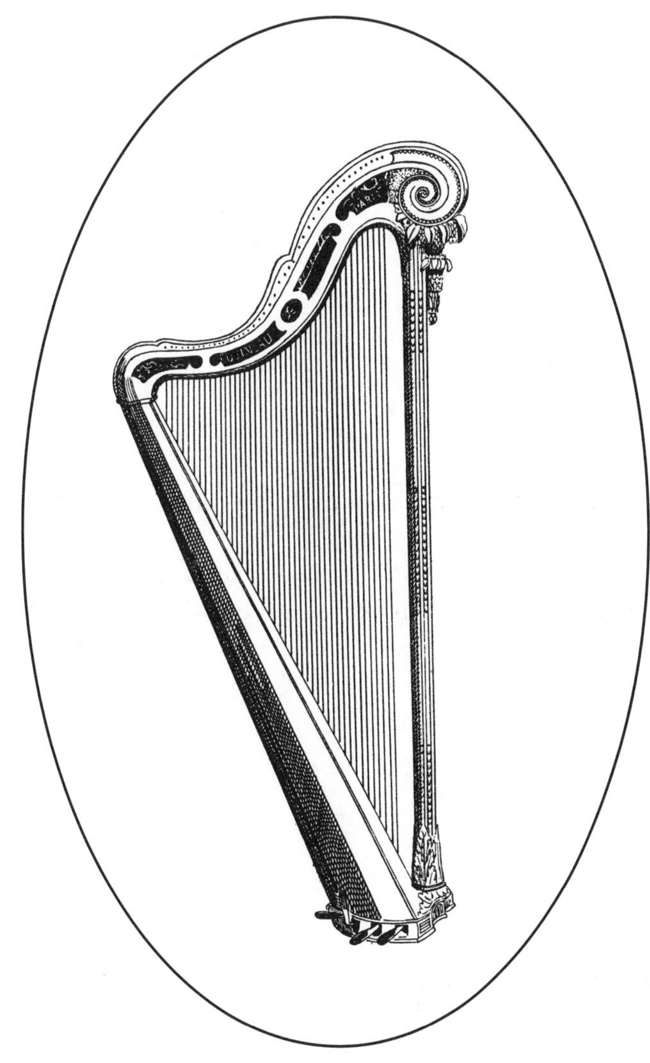

for lever and pedal harp

**I would like to dedicate this book to all of the wonderful people who have been my harp students.
You are my inspiration.**

Special thanks to Liza Rey Butler for pedal markings and other suggestions.

Thank you, also to Molly Hahn, for last minute assistance, and to Forrest Dillon, my partner in music and in life, for all of his knowledge and patient support.

P.O. Box 157, Brunswick, ME 04011

ISBN 0-9628120-8-0

CONTENTS

Introduction

This book is a collection of themes and excerpts selected from the classical repertoire. Many of them will be familiar to you. They are all playable on lever and pedal harps. Many are appropriate to play in church or for weddings. Some of the pieces that are especially effective for processionals include, *St. Anthony Chorale, Largo* from *New World Symphony, Dance of the Spirits, Jupiter* from *The Planets,* and *Voluntary* by Stanley. The last two are my personal favorites. *Ode to Joy* makes a good recessional and *Meditation* from *Thais* and *Choral* by Schumann are good selections for reflective moments. Whether you play the harp as an amateur or professional, harp student or teacher, it is my hope that you will enjoy this book for many years to come.

Lever and Pedal Changes

About half of the pieces in this book have accidentals that require lever or pedal changes. Lever changes are indicated in the score with diamond-headed notes. Pedal changes are written below the score. It may be helpful to highlight or white-out either to make the score easier to read. Accidental markings apply to all of the notes of the same pitch within the same measure.

In some situations, the best time to perform a lever change may be well in advance of the actual note. At other times, damping the note may be necessary to eliminate audible changes. If the tension on your levers is adjustable, loosen them so the action is smooth and quick. It may take a little practice to perform a lever change without missing a beat. Try to work it into the rhythm of the measure so it fits into the flow of the music. It will be easier to remember and will go more smoothly.

Some notes may need to be played by the right hand in order to make the lever change and these directions may be ignored by pedal harpists and played by the left hand as usual.

Glossary

Largo Very slow, broad, and expressive.
Adagio Slow, comfortable.
Andante Moderately slow, walking pace.
Moderato Moderate speed.
Andantino Slightly quicker than Andante.
Allegretto Lightly, a little less fast than Allegro.
Allegro Quick.
Un Poco Piu Mosso A little more animated.
Allegro Risoluto Quick and resolute.
Sostenuto Sustained sound.
Rit. Ritardando, gradual slowing.
A Tempo In time.
Gliss Glissando, sweep one finger across the strings in the direction indicated.
+ Play using thumb with flat palm, damping previous note as you go.
⌖ Muffle or damp strings.

Menuet in G Major

Arr: Deborah Friou

Carl Philipp Emanuel Bach
(1714-1788)

Choral

Arr: Deborah Friou

Robert Schumann
(1810-1856)

Minuet

from ***Don Giovanni***

Arr: Deborah Friou

Wolfgang Amadeus Mozart
(1756-1791)

Musetta's Waltz

from ***La Boheme***

Arr: Deborah Friou

Giacomo Puccini
(1858-1924)

p
R.H.
R.H.
slower
a tempo
slower
a tempo
L.H.
R.H.
mf
slower
L.H.
pp

La Donna E Mobile

from ***Rigoletto***

Arr: Deborah Friou

Giuseppe Verdi
(1813-1901)

p
F♯
G♯
f
mp
pp
cresc.
f
G♯

Variations On A Theme Of Haydn

St. Anthony Chorale

Arr: Deborah Friou

Johannes Brahms
(1833-1897)

Andante

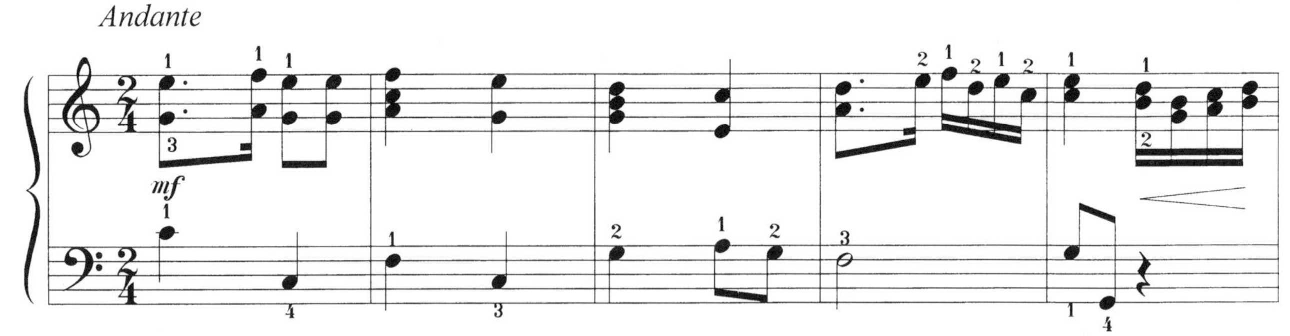

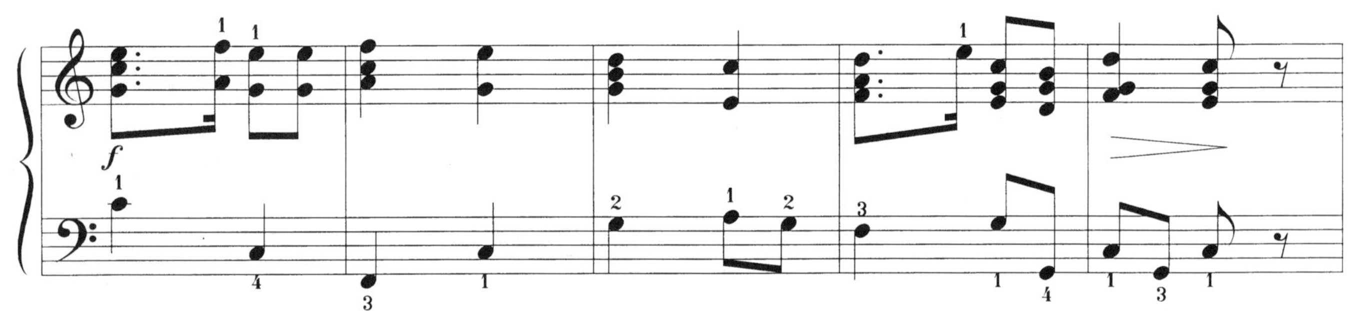

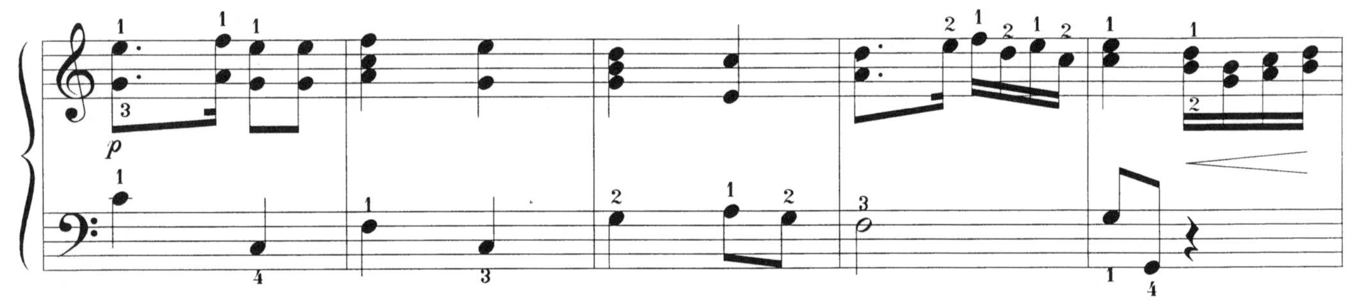

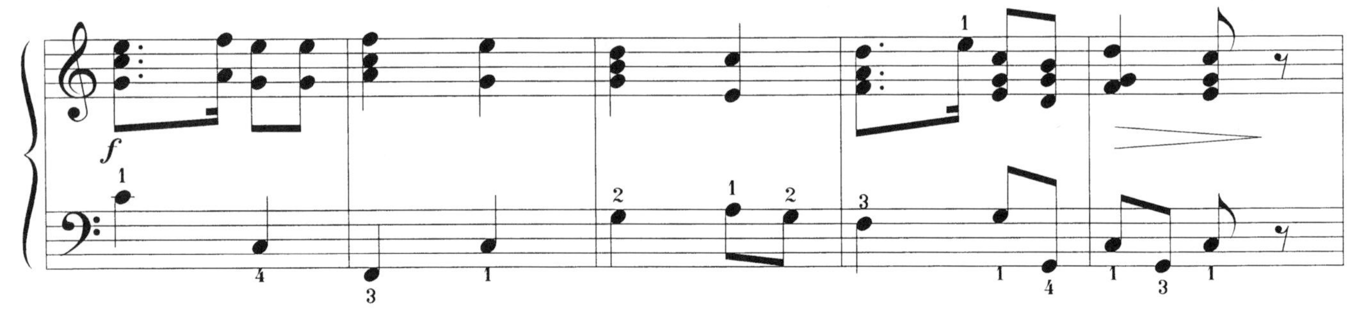

p
pp
f
decresc.
p

Menuet al Rovescio

Arr: Deborah Friou

Franz Joseph Haydn
(1732-1809)

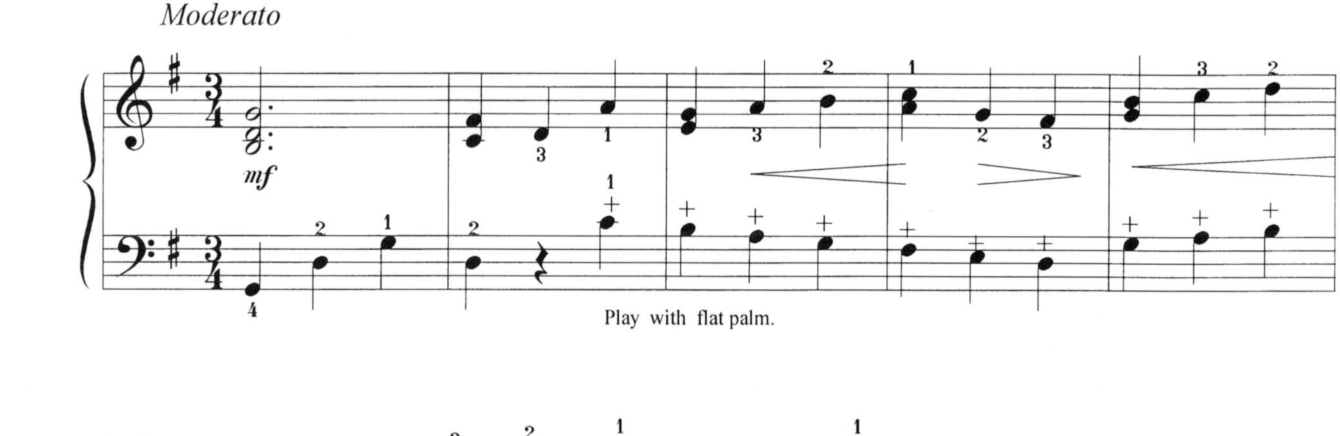

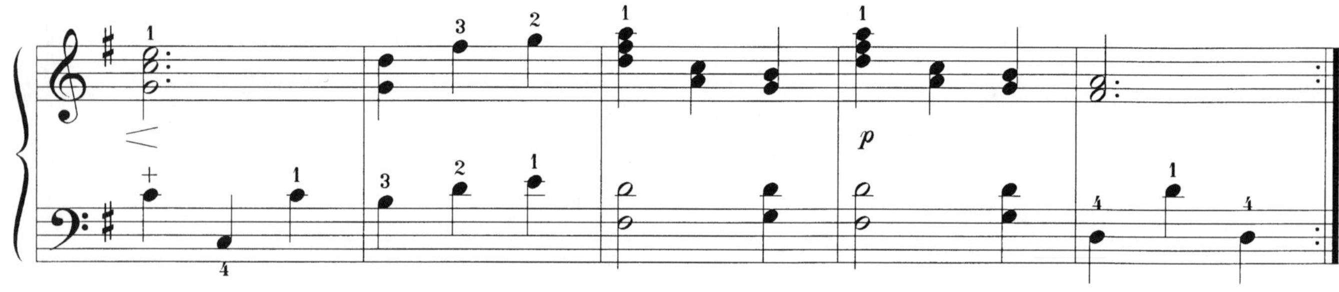

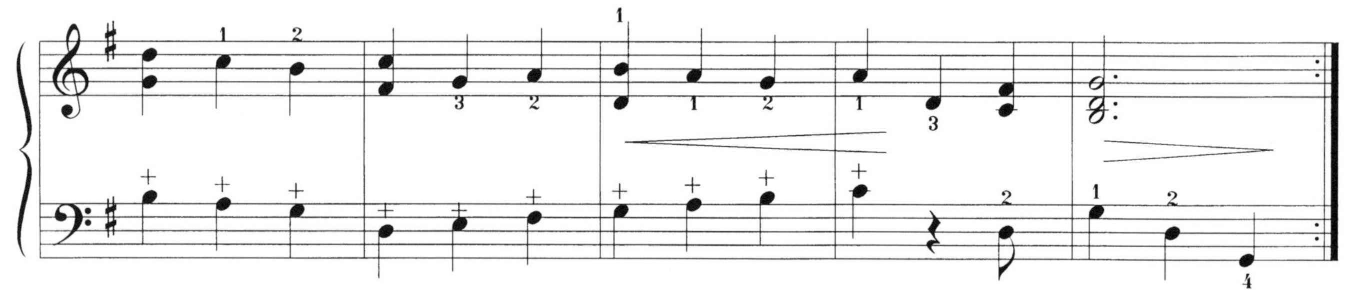

Many of the classical composers enjoyed incorporating musical jokes and puzzles into their compositions. This is a "reversible menuet". The second and fourth sections are backwards versions of the first and third.

Trio

Lullaby

Arr: Deborah Friou

Johannes Brahms
(1833-1897)

ppp

Waltz

Arr: Deborah Friou

Johannes Brahms
(1833-1897)

Sonatina in G

Arr: Deborah Friou

Franz Joseph Haydn
(1732-1809)

Polovtsian Dance

from ***Prince Igor***

Arr: Deborah Friou

Alexander Borodin
(1833-1887)

Moderato

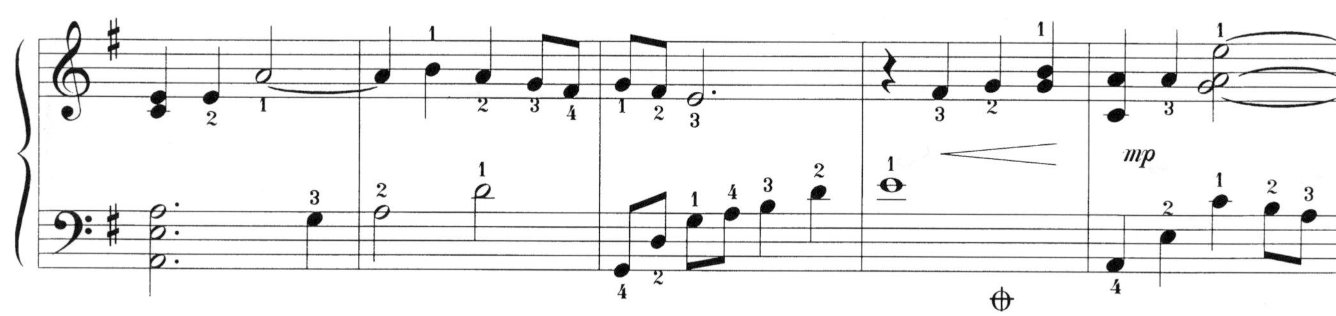

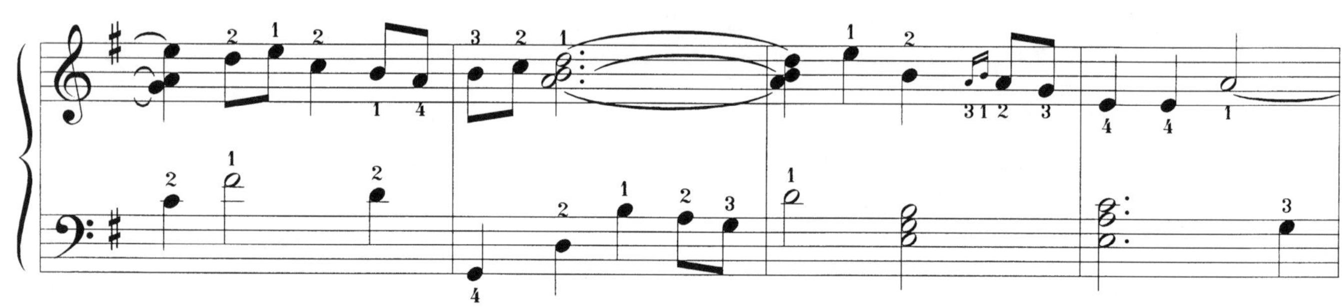

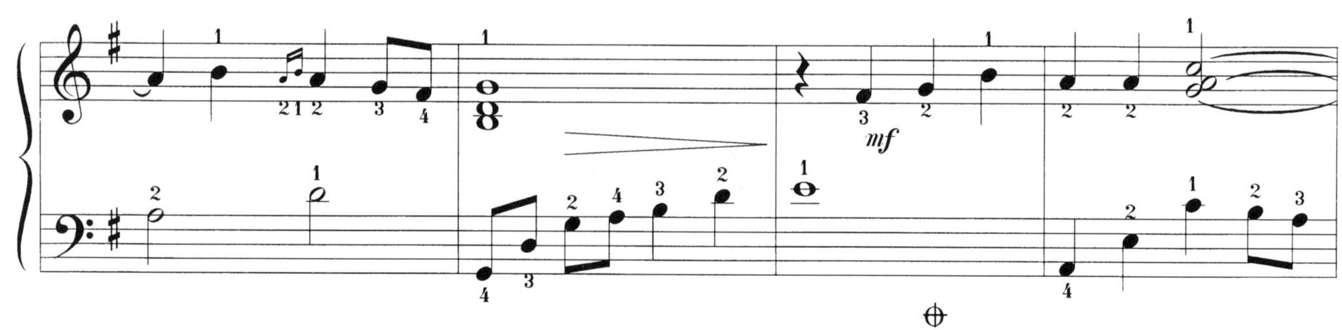

p
pp

The Blue Danube

Arr: Deborah Friou

Johann Strauss
(1825-1899)

Fine
p
G♯
f
G♮
p
f
F♯
1.
2.
p
p
F♮

D.C. al Fine

Emperor Waltz

Arr: Deborah Friou

Johann Strauss
(1825-1899)

rit.
a tempo
mp

f

Pavane

Arr: Deborah Friou

Gabriel Faure
(1845-1924)

p
F♮
rit.
F♯
D♯

Dance of the Spirits

from ***Orfeo ed Euridice***

Arr: Deborah Friou

Christoph Willibald Gluck
(1714-1787)

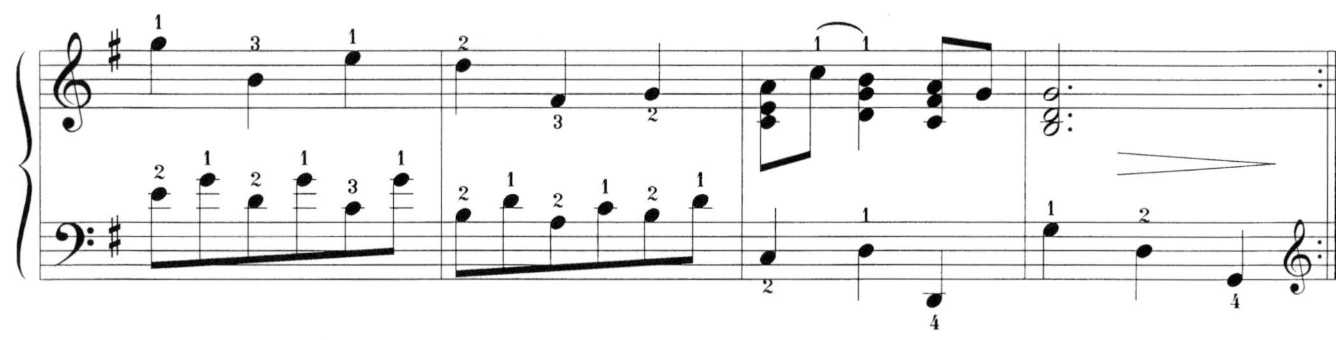

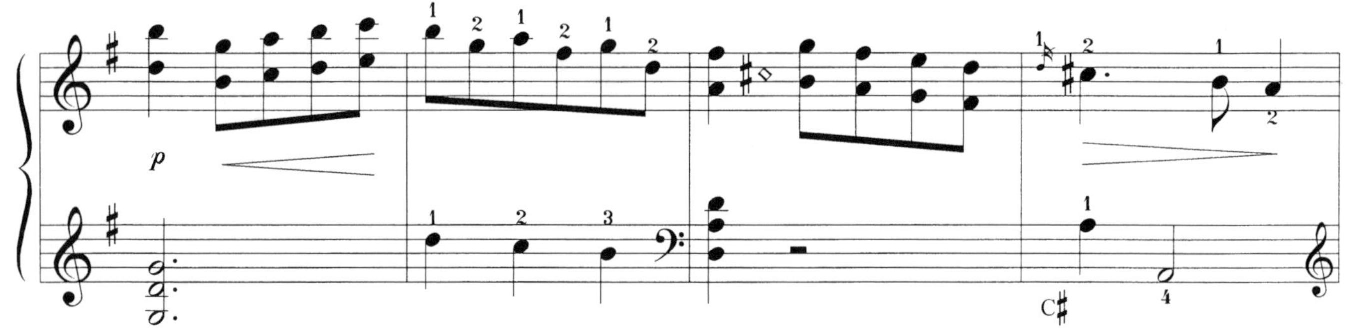

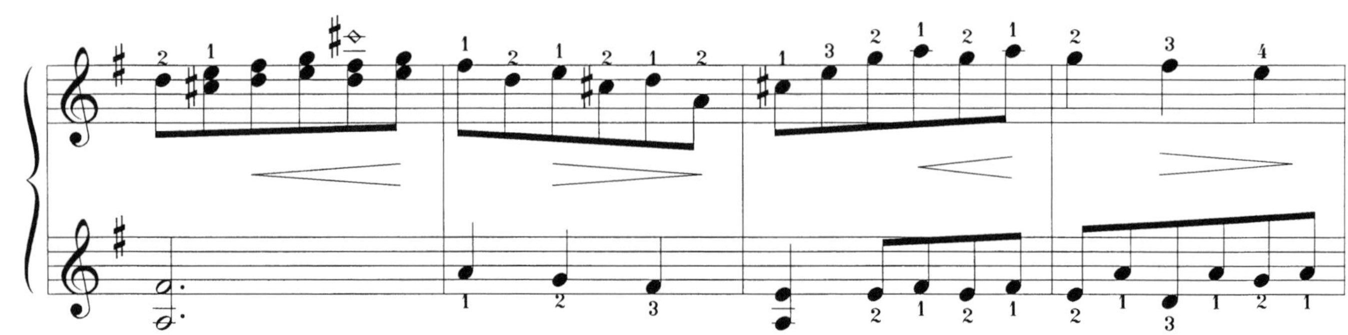

cresc.
f
C♮
p
mf

Skater's Waltz

Arr: Deborah Friou

Emile Waldteufel
(1837-1915)

2.
mf
rit.
a tempo

D.S. al Fine

Trout Quintet

Theme

Arr: Deborah Friou

Franz Schubert
(1797-1828)

On Wings of Song

Arr: Deborah Friou

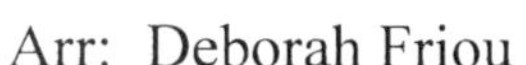

Felix Mendelssohn
(1809-1847)

Andante

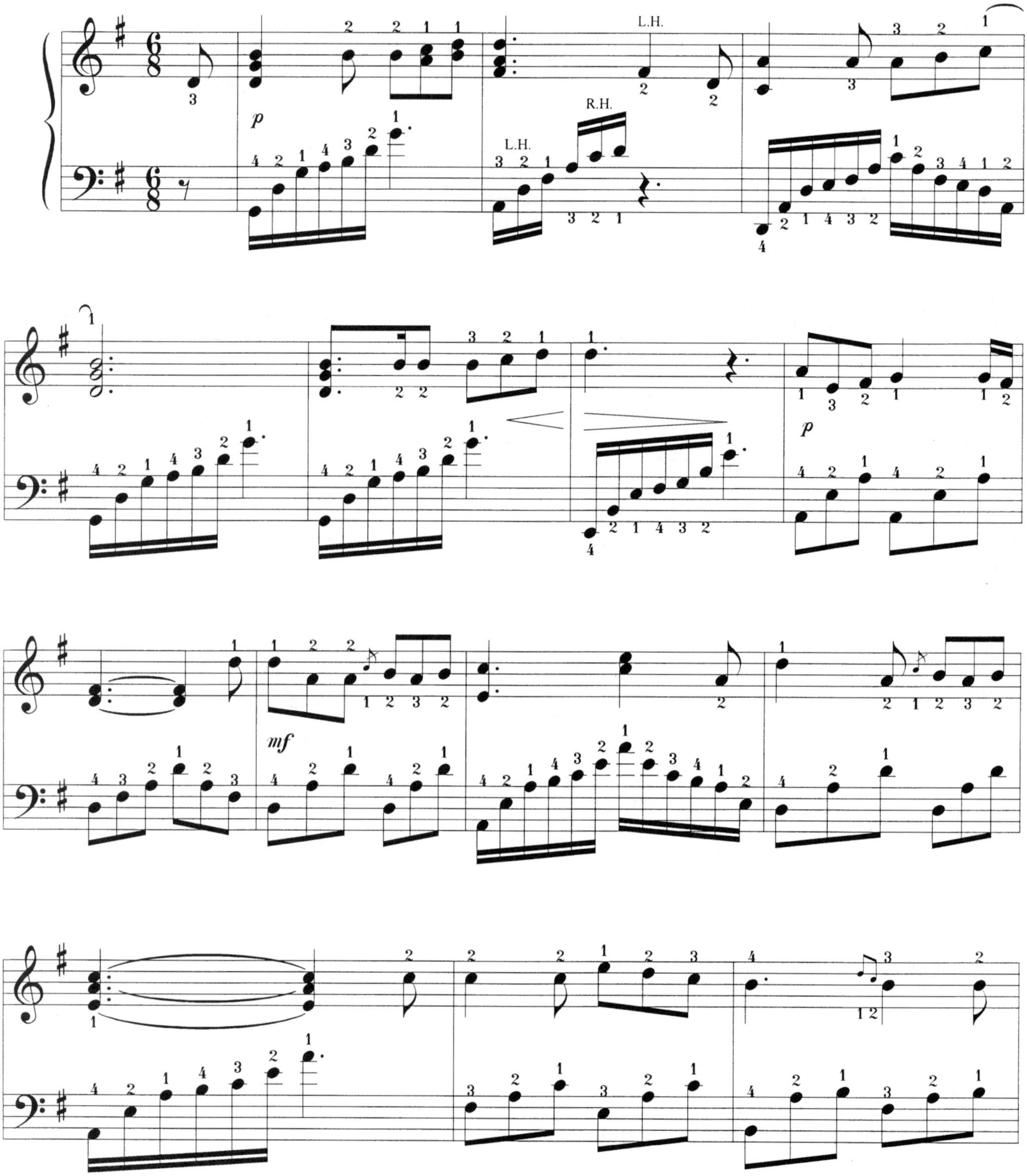

p
p
pp
ppp

Barcarolle

from ***Tales of Hoffman***

Arr: Deborah Friou

Jacques Offenbach
(1819-1880)

mf
mp
dim.
pp

Jupiter

From ***The Planets***

Arr: Deborah Friou

Gustav Holst
(1874-1934)

mf
ff
mf

O, My Beloved Father

from ***Gianni Schicchi***

Arr: Deborah Friou

Giacomo Puccini
(1858-1924)

pp
R.H.

Eine Kleine Nachtmusik

***Theme** - First Movement*

Arr: Deborah Friou

Wolfgang Amadeus Mozart
(1756-1791)

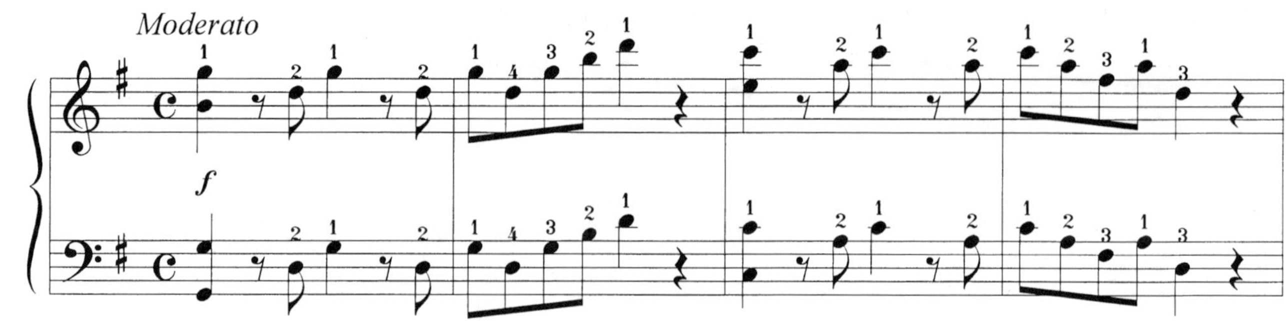

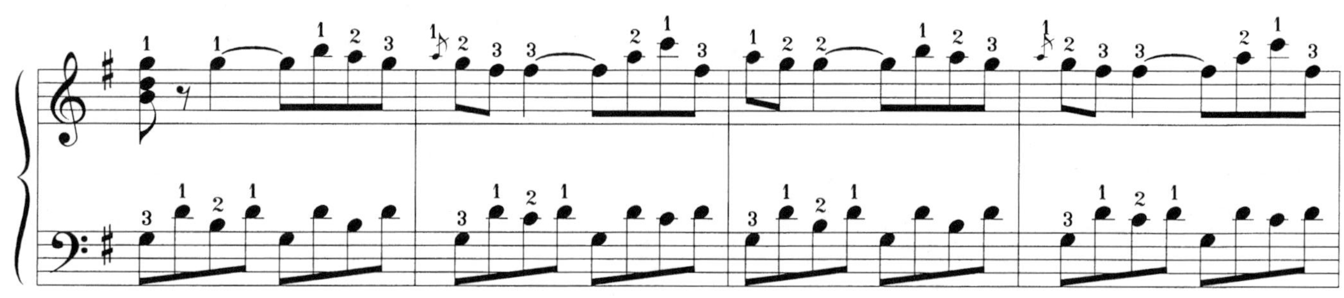

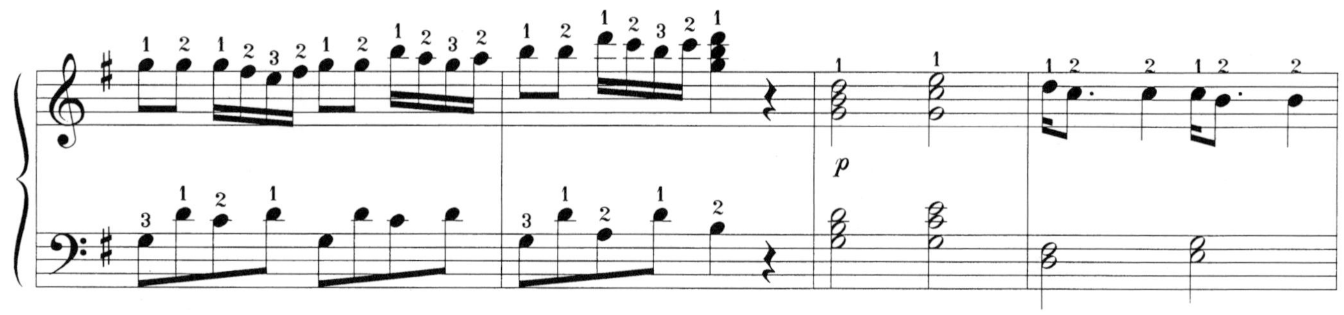

C♯
f
C♮
p

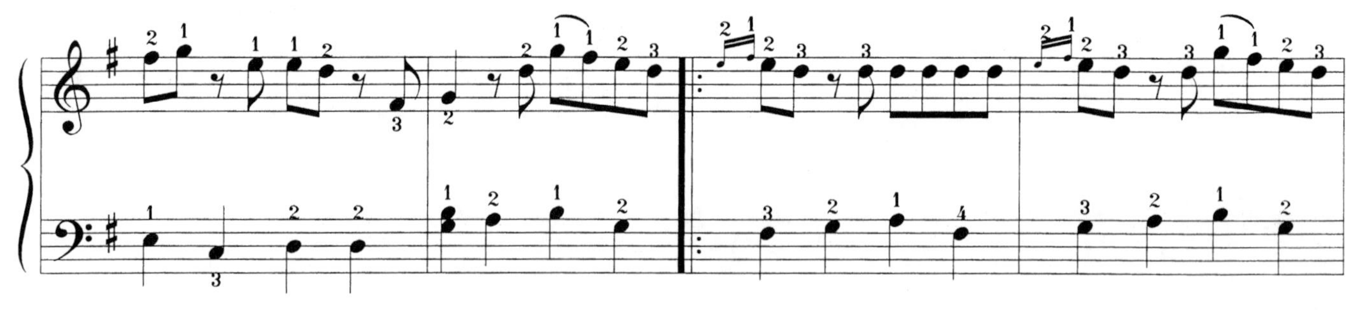

f
G♯ ♮

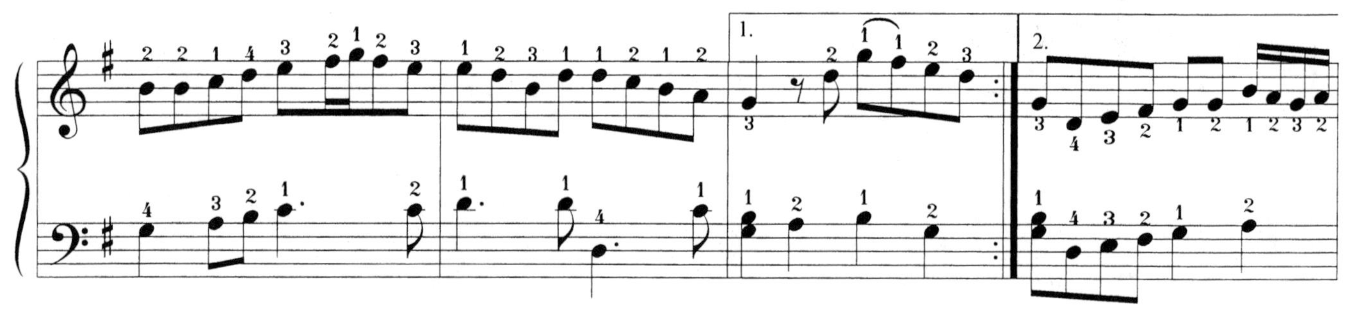

1.
2.

Damp strings first.
p
C♯ D♯
C♮ D♮

C♯-----♮
cresc.
f

Eine Kleine Nachtmusik

***Romance**-Second Movement*

Arr: Deborah Friou

Wolfgang Amadeus Mozart
(1756-1791)

Melodie

from *Album for the Young*

Arr: Deborah Friou

Robert Schumann
(1810-1856)

Voluntary

Arr: Deborah Friou

John Stanley
(1712-1786)

cresc.
G♯
G♮
cresc.

Fur Elise

Arr: Deborah Friou

Ludwig van Beethoven
(1770-1827)

Andante
Lever Harps fix:

pp

D♯ ---------------- ♮

G♯

D♯ ---------------- ♮

1.

2.

D♯

G♮

mf

R.H.
L.H.
R.H.
L.H.
R.H.
L.H.
R.H.
p
rit.
pp
a tempo
D♯
D♮
G♯
D♯
♮
1.
2.
rit.
G♮

Menuet

Arr: Deborah Friou

Franz Schubert
(1797-1828)

Trio
p
1.
2.
mf
F♯
p
D.C. al Fine
(1st time only)

Clair De Lune

Arr: Deborah Friou

Claude Debussy
(1862-1918)

Alternate note for pedal harpists.
A♭
A♮
dim.
rit.
D♯
L.H.
R.H.
R.H.
ppp

Humoreske

Arr: Deborah Friou

Antonin Dvorak
(1841-1904)

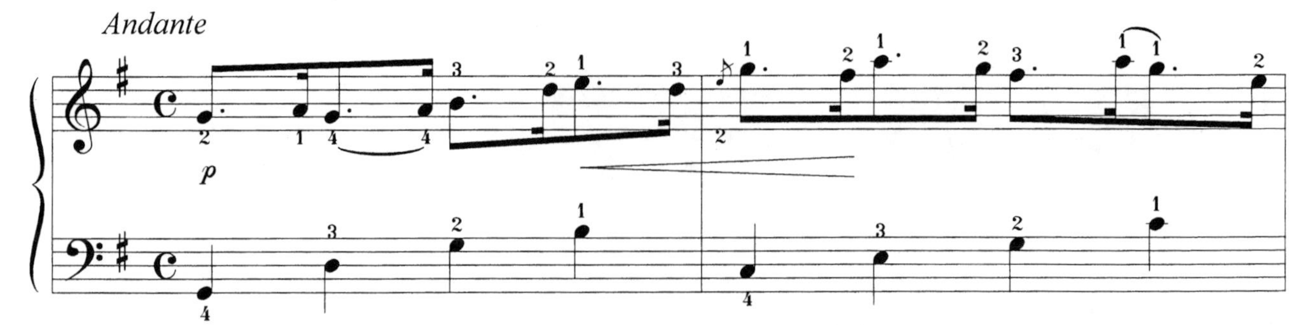

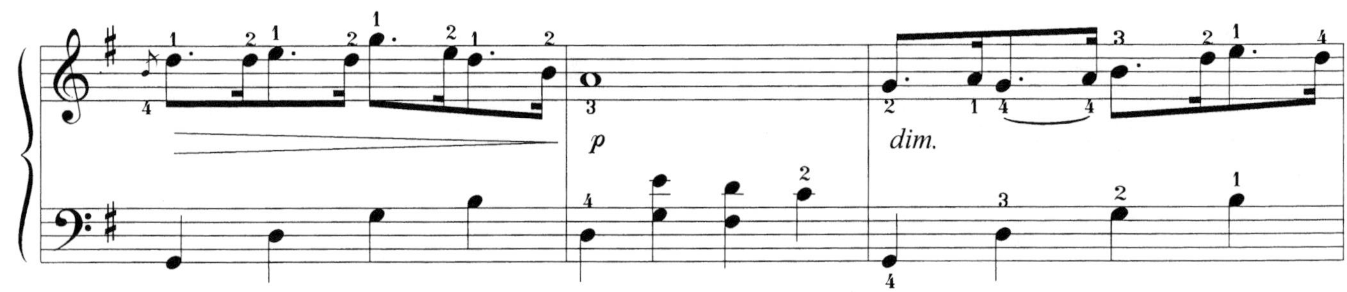

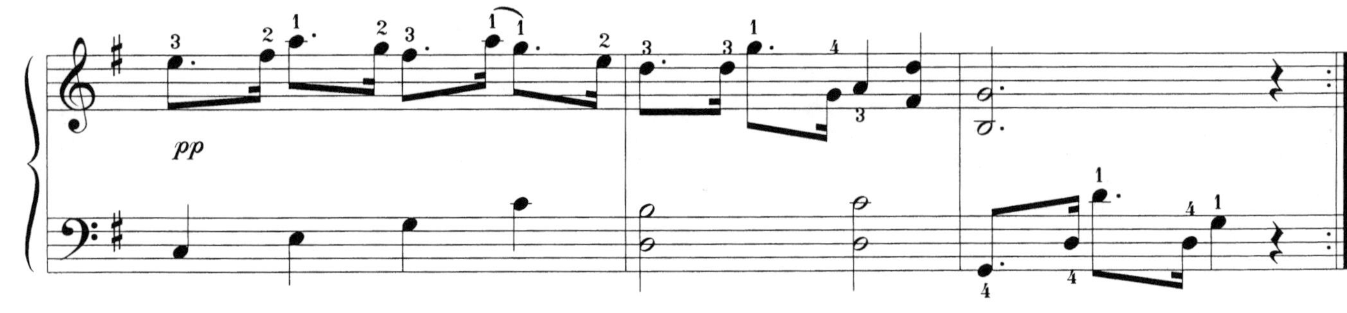

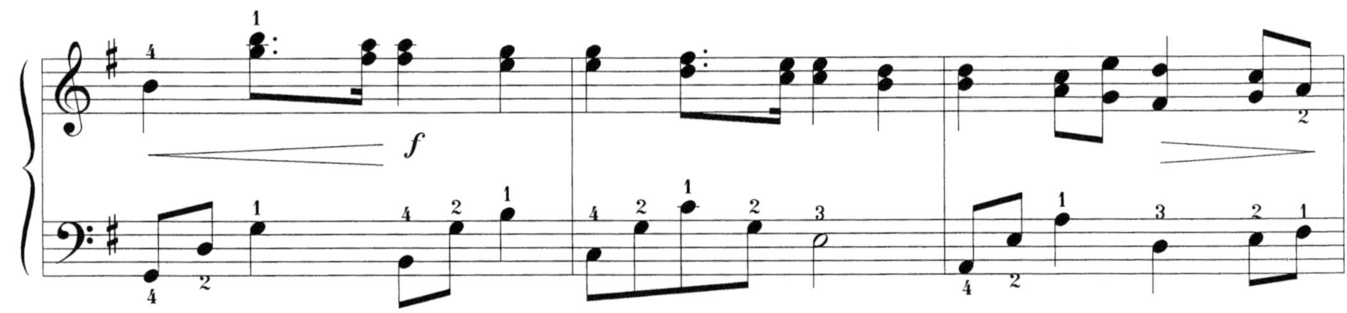

* Lever harps tuned in C can substitute A♯ for B♭.

Caprice

from ***Alceste***

Arr: Deborah Friou

Christoph Willibald Gluck
(1714-1787)

f
ff
mf
pp
p
mf
f

p
f

New World Symphony Themes

Arr: Deborah Friou

Antonin Dvorak
(1841-1904)

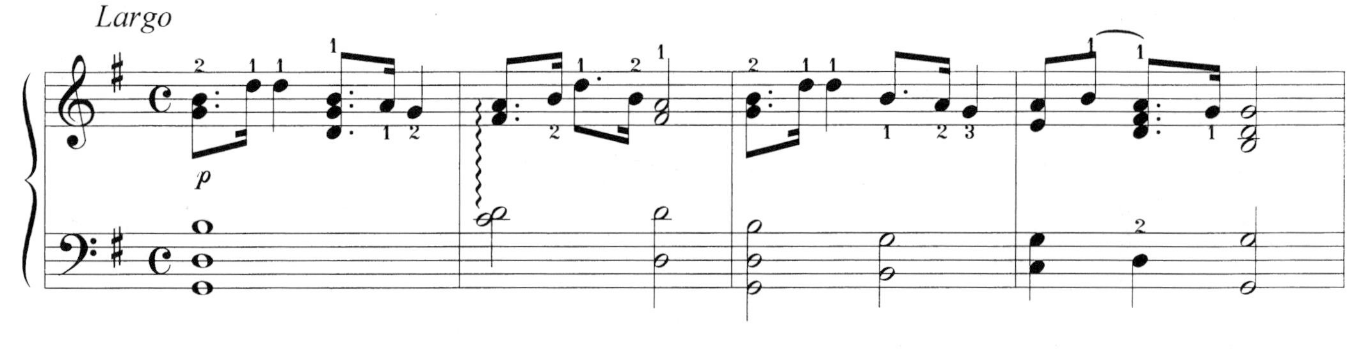
Largo
p

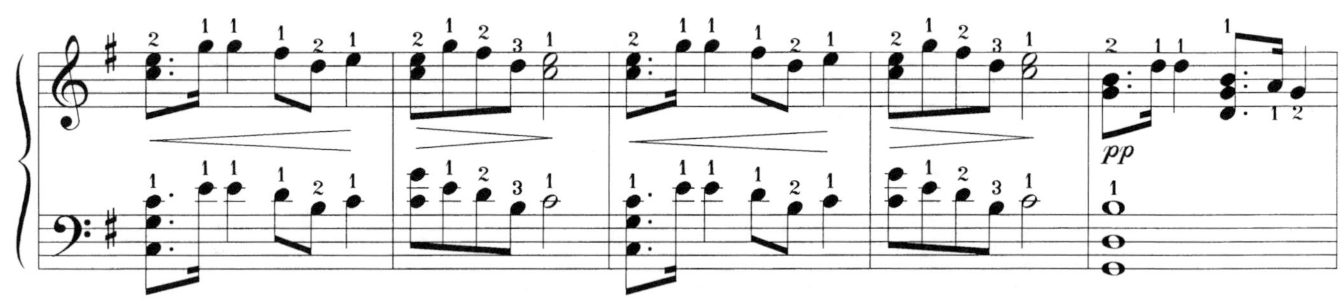
pp

f

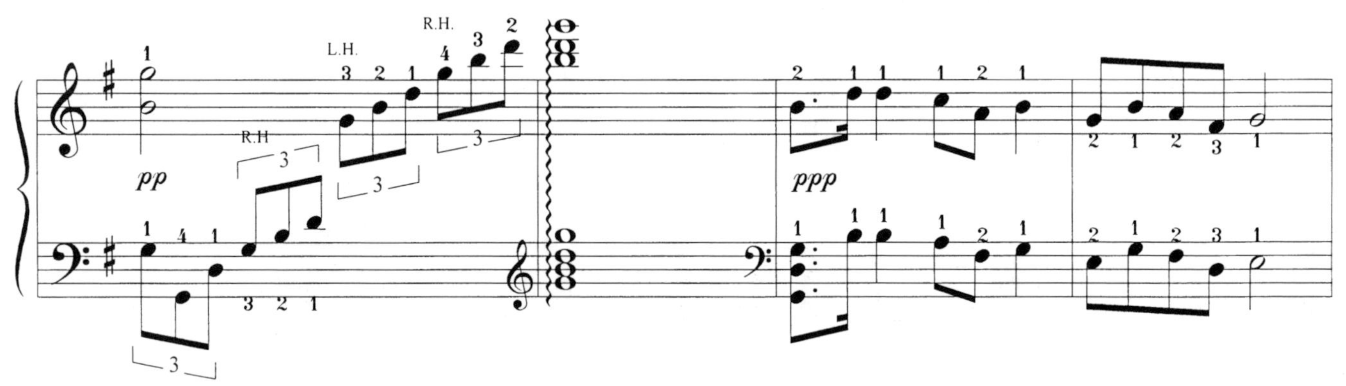
pp
R.H
L.H.
R.H.
ppp

cresc.

dim.

ppp

p

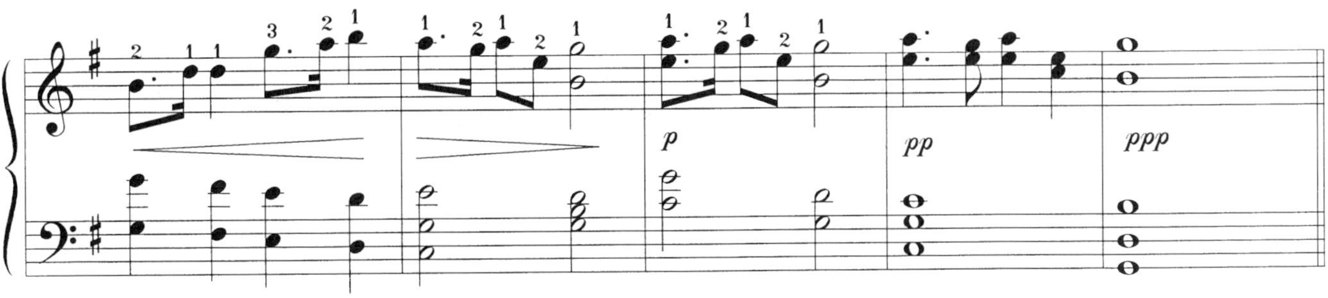

Un poco piu mosso
Lever Harps Fix:
pp
f
p
cresc.
f
pp
cresc.
mf
dim.
F♮
pp
decresc.
ppp
F♯

Allegro risoluto
mf
f
D♯
D♮
1.
2.
ff
G♯

Waltz

Arr: Deborah Friou

Franz Schubert
(1797-1828)

Waltz

Arr: Deborah Friou

Franz Schubert

Meditation

from *Thais*

Arr: Deborah Friou
For Lever Harps tuned in E♭.

Jules Massenet
(1842-1912)

Andante

pp

G♯------♮

rall.

a tempo

Damp string first.

ppp

B♭ ----------♮

f

F♮ F♯ G♯ G♮

p

cresc.

rall.
a tempo
R.H.
p
C♯
f
C♮
E♭
mf
E♮
dim.
R.H.
L.H.
p
D♯
D♮
pp

Meditation

from *Thais*

Arr: Deborah Friou
For Lever Harps in a C tuning.

Jules Massenet
(1842-1912)

rall.
a tempo
p
R.H.
f
mf
dim.
L.H.
pp

Moonlight Sonata

Theme

Arr: Deborah Friou

Ludwig van Beethoven
(1770-1827)

Adagio sostenuto

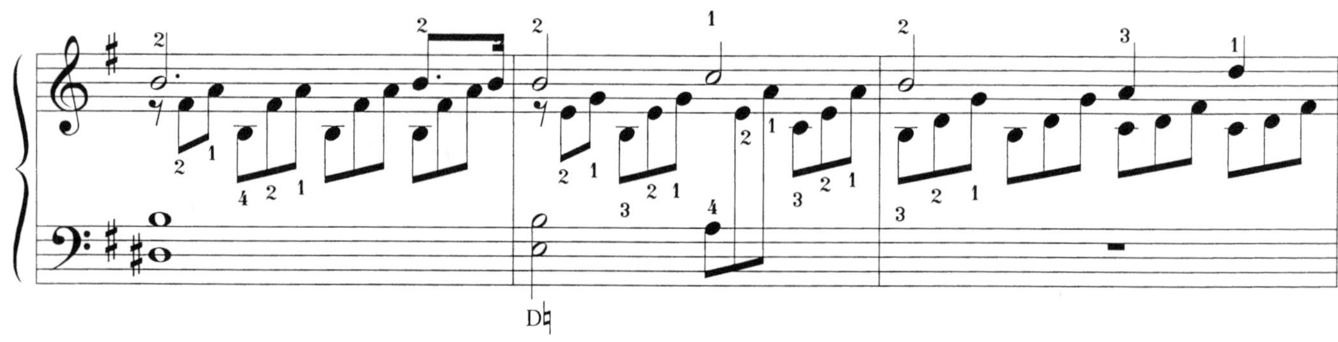

L.H.
p
F♮
pp
G♯
L.H.
L.H.
R.H.
L.H. .
L.H.
L.H.
R.H.
F♯
G♮
D♮
D♯

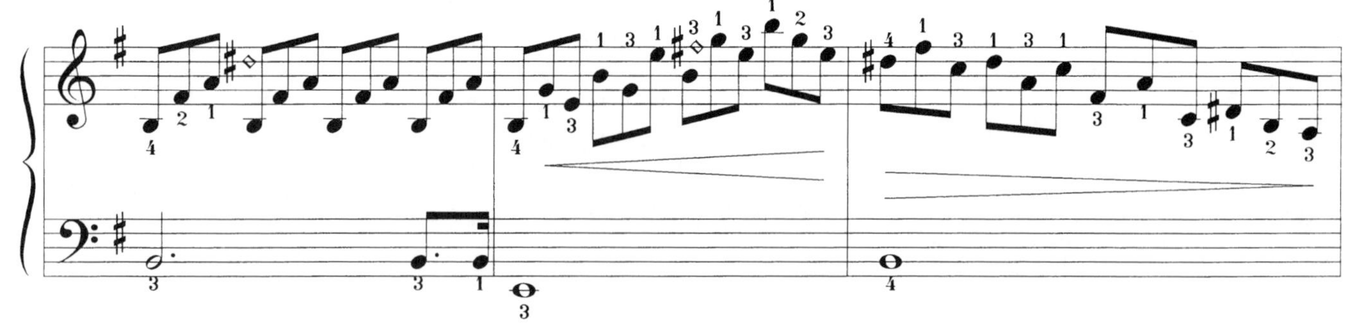

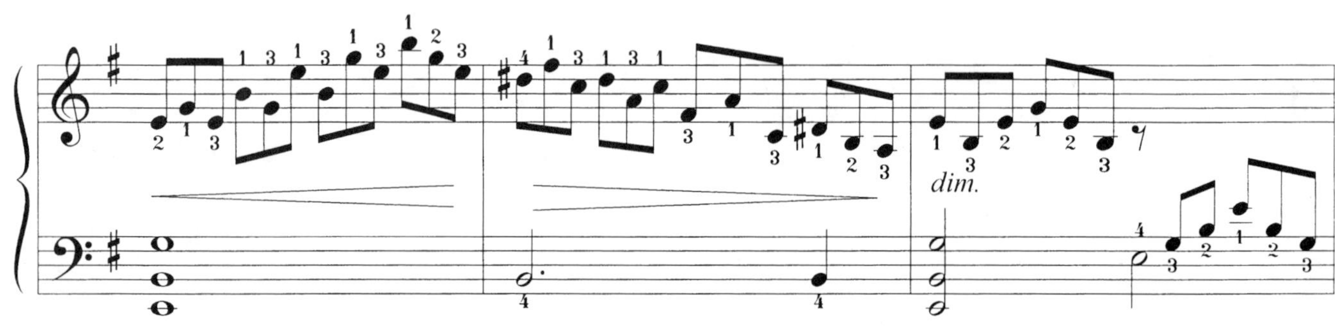
dim.

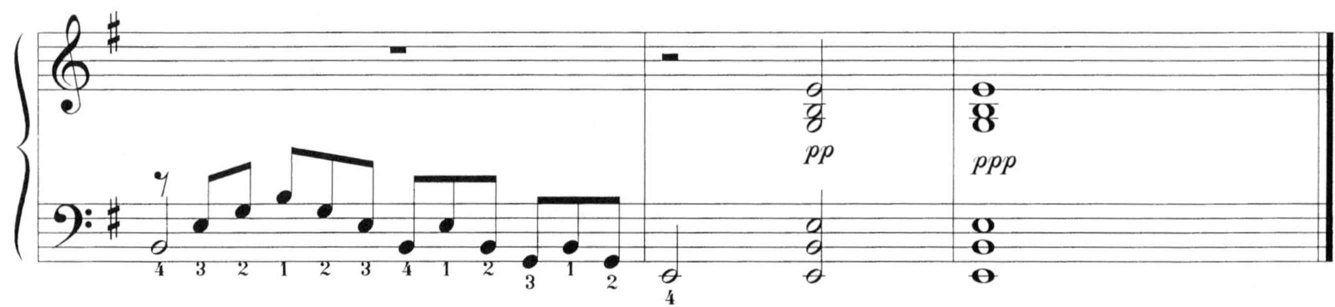
pp
ppp

Ode to Joy

Arr: Deborah Friou

Ludwig van Beethoven
(1770-1827)

Allegro

p

cresc.

p

cresc.

p

Play with flat palm.
cresc.
p
cresc.
p

p
1.
2.
cresc.
p
C♮---------------------♯
C♮---------------------♯

Minuet

Arr: Deborah Friou
For Lever Harps tuned with B♭.

Luigi Boccherini
(1743-1806)

Minuet

Arr: Deborah Friou
For Lever Harps in a C tuning.

Luigi Boccherini
(1743-1806)

About Foreign Lands and People

Arr: Deborah Friou

Robert Shumann
(1810-1856)

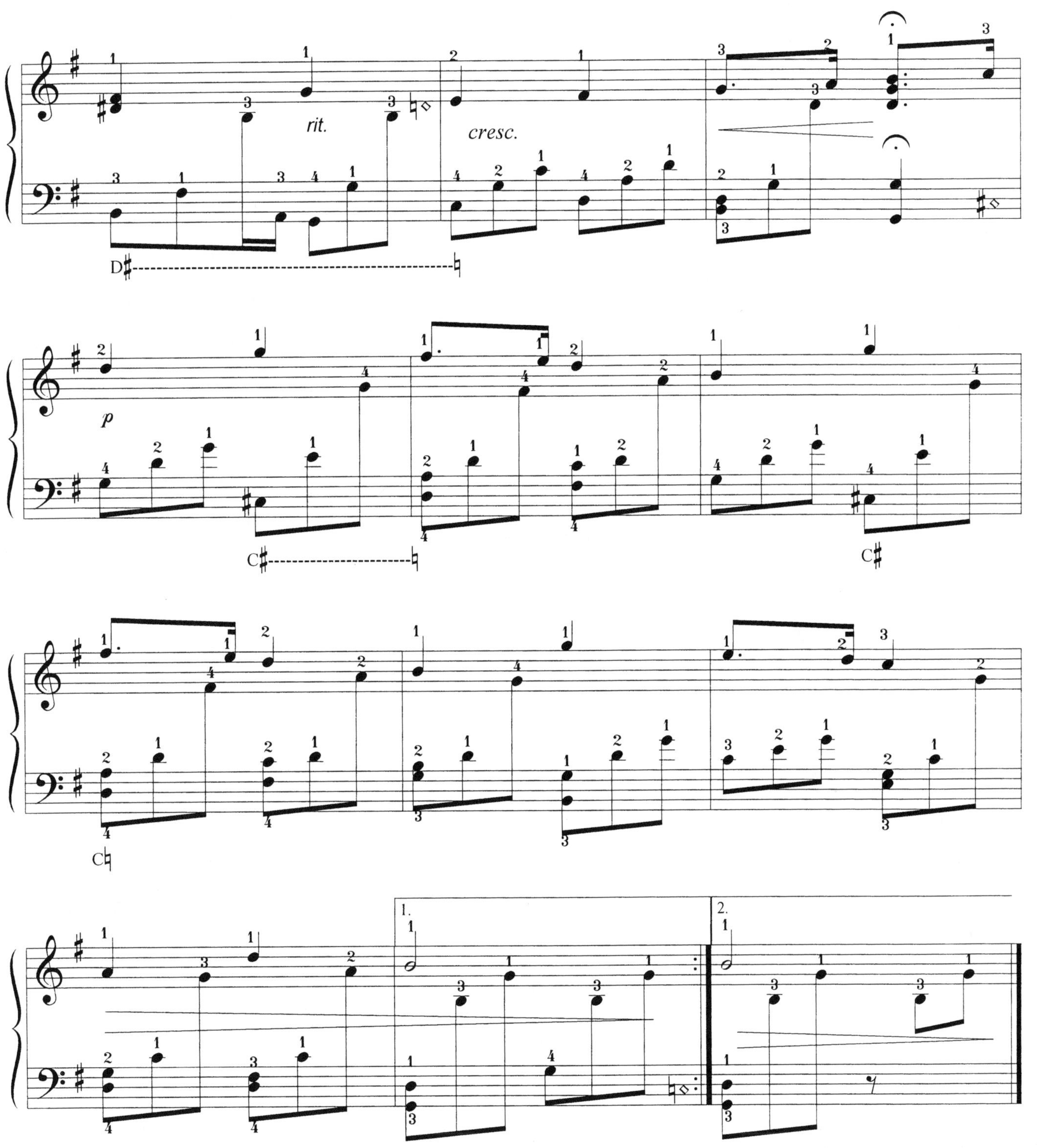
rit.
cresc.
D♯
p
C♯
C♯
C♮
1.
2.

Sonata I in C

Arr: Deborah Friou

Wolfgang Amadeus Mozart
(1756-1791)

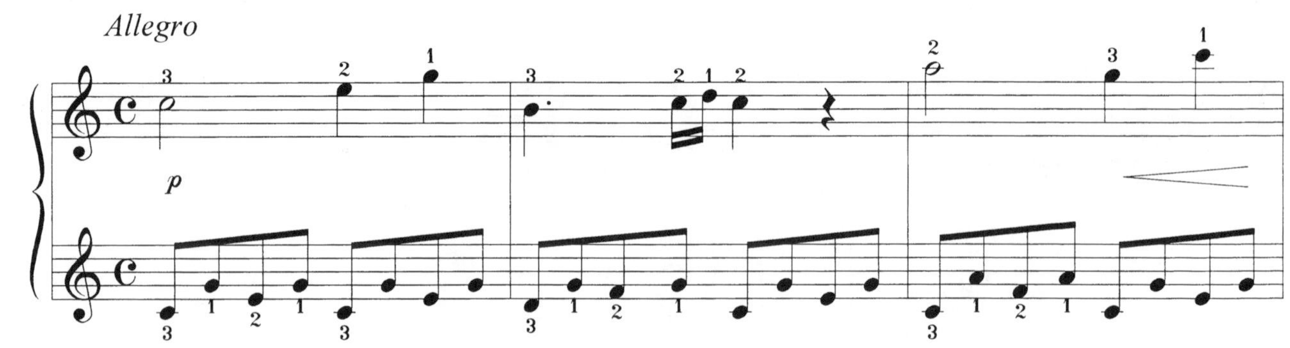

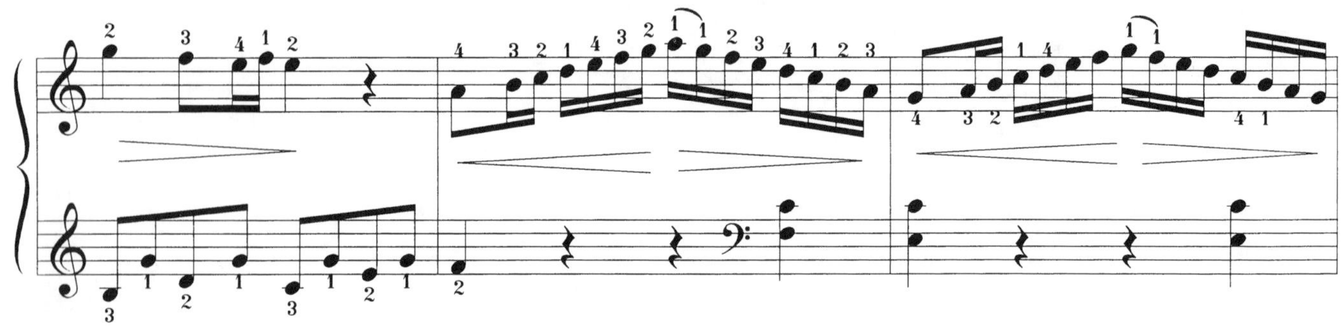

p
cresc.
R.H.
G♯
D♯
f
G♮
D♮

Sonata No. 9

Theme

Arr: Deborah Friou

Wolfgang Amadeus Mozart
(1756-1791)

Serenade

from ***String Quartet in F***

Arr: Deborah Friou

Franz Joseph Haydn
(1732-1809)

mf
p
mf
p

Sonatina

Arr: Deborah Friou

Ludwig van Beethoven
(1770-1827)

F♮ ♯

mf

p

f

Allegretto

mf
p
mf
f
C♯
Fix A♯
Fix A♮
p
cresc.
f
rit.
mp
a tempo
C♮
A♯-----A♮
C♯-----------------------♮
F♮
p
F♯
mf
f

The Happy Farmer

Arr: Deborah Friou

Robert Schumann
(1810-1856)

La Paloma

Arr: Deborah Friou

Sebastian Iradier
(1809-1865)

F♯
p
glis.
mf
F♮
f
mf
p

Wild Rider

Arr: Deborah Friou

Robert Schumann
(1810-1856)